That is My Dream!

A picture book of Langston Hughes's "Dream Variation," illustrated by Daniel Miyares

schwartz & wade books · new york

To fling my arms wide

In some place of the sun,

To whirl and to dance

Till the white day is done.

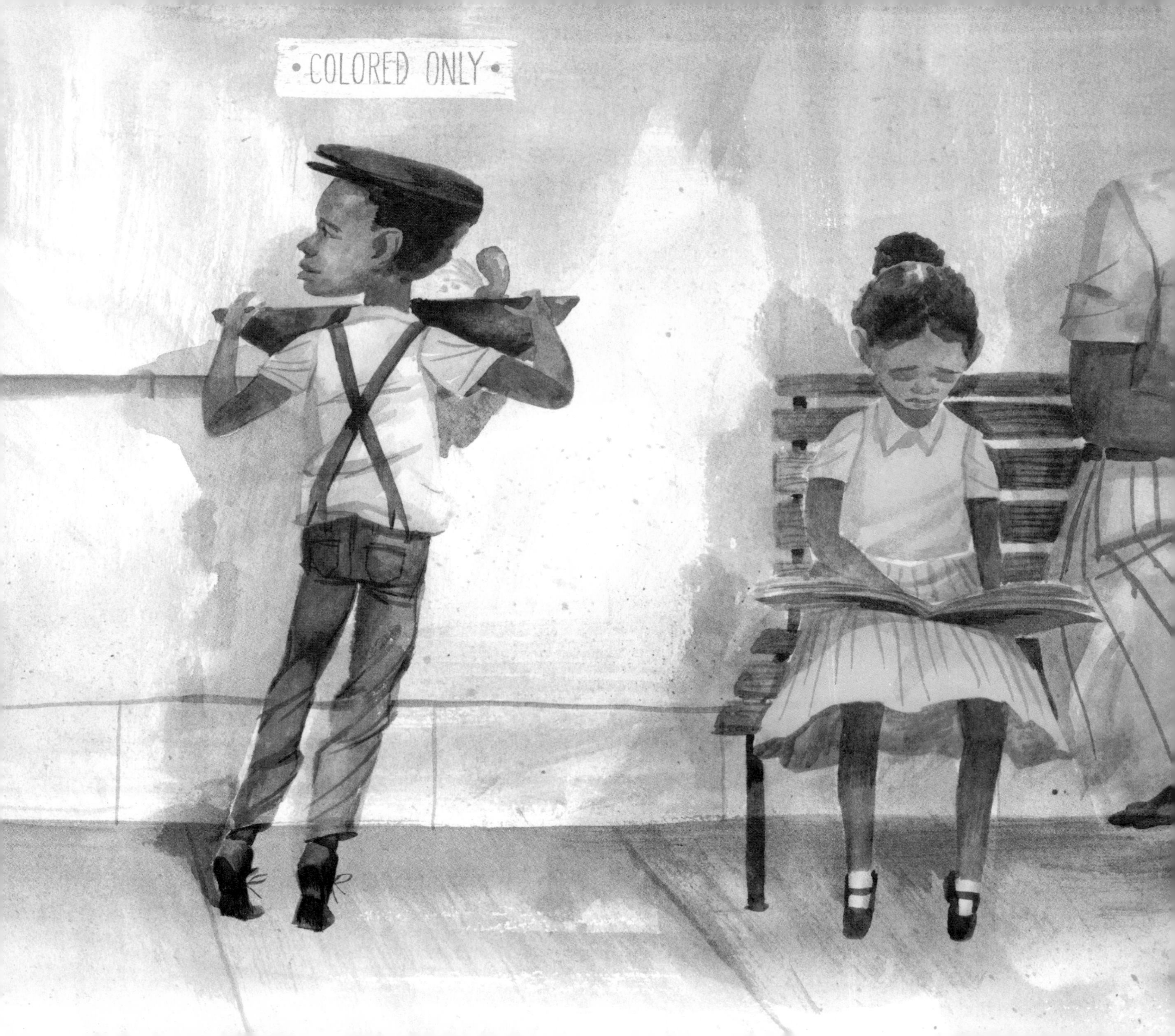
COLORED ONLY

Then rest at cool evening

Beneath a tall tree

While night comes on gently,

Dark like me—

That is my dream!

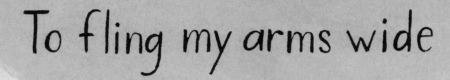
To fling my arms wide

In the face of the sun,

Dance!
Whirl!
Whirl!

Till the quick day is done.

Rest at pale evening...

A tall, slim tree ...

Night coming tenderly

Black like me.

For L.H. —D.M.

Illustrator's Note

I first encountered the poetry of Langston Hughes in my high school English class. We were studying the Harlem Renaissance and the role Hughes played in it. His work showed me a version of the American experience that I had never seen before, and I was profoundly moved. For the first time, I understood the raw power of poetry—its ability to peel back a façade and reveal deep truths that may be hard for us to see.

This was a huge deal for my teenage self, growing up in Simpsonville, South Carolina. It's the reason I wanted to share Hughes's "Dream Variation" as a picture book. In the poem (as I interpret it), Hughes powerfully contrasts a day smothered by inequality with one of bright hope. My wish is that this story be a catalyst for empathy, just as it was for me—especially among our youngest readers. I've called my version *That Is My Dream!*—using a line that lies at the very heart of the poem—in an attempt to make it more inviting to this audience.

I have two young children at home, and my dream for them is that they'll always value listening more than judging and understanding more than righteousness.

Text copyright © 1926 by Alfred A. Knopf, a division of Penguin Random House LLC.
Copyright renewed 1954 by Langston Hughes
Jacket art and interior illustrations copyright © 2017 by Daniel Miyares
All rights reserved. Published in the United States by Schwartz & Wade Books, an imprint of Random House Children's Books, a division of Penguin Random House LLC, New York.
The text of this book was first published as the poem "Dream Variation" in 1924 and subsequently included in the collection *The Weary Blues* published by Alfred A. Knopf, in 1926.
Schwartz & Wade Books and the colophon are trademarks of Penguin Random House LLC.
"Dream Variation" by Langston Hughes reprinted by arrangement with Alfred A. Knopf, New York, a division of Penguin Random House LLC.

Visit us on the Web! randomhousekids.com
Educators and librarians, for a variety of teaching tools, visit us at RHTeachersLibrarians.com
Library of Congress Cataloging-in-Publication Data is available upon request.
ISBN 978-0-399-55017-1 (hc) —
ISBN 978-0-399-55018-8 (lib. bdg.) —
ISBN 978-0-399-55019-5 (ebook)
The text of this book is hand lettered by the artist.
The illustrations were rendered in gouache on Strathmore paper.
MANUFACTURED IN CHINA
10 9 8 7 6 5 4 3 2 1

First Edition